Ordinary Days with an Extraordinary God

Ordinary Days with an Extraordinary God

Prayerables II

by
IRENE HARRELL

WORD BOOKS, Publishers
Waco, Texas

To half a dozen Harrells—
Tommy
Alice
Dino
Susan
'Guerite
&
Maria

Contents

Preface

"From the one man he created all races of men, and made them live over the whole earth. He himself fixed beforehand the exact times and the limits of the places where they would live. He did this so that they would look for him, and perhaps find him as they felt around for him. Yet God is actually not far from any one of us; for 'In him we live and move and are.' "

Acts 17:26–28 (TEV)

As surely as we have felt around for God we *have* found him everywhere, in all of life. This truth has become increasingly clear to me in the preparation of *Ordinary Days with an Extraordinary God*. I pray that it may be an instrument for heightening your awareness that God *is indeed* closer than breathing, nearer than hands and feet.

Would you be happy? Hear William Law, writing in the eighteenth century:

"As there is no foundation for comfort in the enjoyments of this life, but in the assurance that a wise and good God governeth the world, so the more we find God in everything, the more we apply to Him in every place, the more we look up to Him in all our actions, the more we conform to His will, the more we act according to His wisdom, and imitate His goodness, by so much more do we enjoy God, partake of the divine nature, and heighten and increase all that is happy and comfortable in human life."

Kee—rash! Crash!

The day of their calamity is at hand.

Deuteronomy 32:35 (KJV)

Four pictures of perfect innocence, one a shade paler than the other three. That's what greeted my eyes when I raced upstairs, heart in my mouth, after hearing a tremendous crash and then stark silence. The children shared a brief second of loyalty and then began talking all at one time.

"It was all Dino's fault."

"He didn't mean to."

"Mama, you shouldn't—"

"I was just trying to get my monkey—"

Relieved to find everyone alive and in one piece, I followed their eyes. All four pair of them were riveted on the closed double doors of the boys' closet. I knew that was where I'd find the trouble. Why else would the doors be

11

closed when despite my nagging they were invariably standing open, revealing their Fibber McGee contents to anyone who passed by? I nudged one knob, gingerly. Both doors crept open then, besieging my ears with a further clatter, as clothes, coat hangers, and toys settled into a precarious heap.

Somehow, the seven-foot-long, heavy, galvanized clothes pole had come loose from its sturdy brackets, letting down the deluge of wearing apparel and empty hangers onto muddy shoes and scattered toys on the floor. You'd have sworn that nothing less than a team of elephants trying to chin themselves could have created such havoc. I knew I'd never unearth the whole truth of the affair buried among the conflicting affirmations and denials of the four conspirators.

Too tired for another explosion that day, I wearily picked up the rumpled things, got the clothes pole rehung, and put everything back in orderly fashion, confident that whatever that particular trick was would not be tried again—until another day.

Later I wondered how just getting one small stuffed monkey down from a shelf could have caused such a catastrophe.

Forgive me, Lord, for the confusions I cause, the messes I create, in my efforts to do some small thing. Forgive me for the excuses I make, the blamings I attempt, when I have taken no heed of the possible consequences of some rash action. Help me to undo the troubles I've caused and restore things as they ought to be. And make me forgiving of my children as you must be forgiving of me. For your love's sake. AMEN.

The Unwelcomed

But Jesus said, Suffer little children, and forbid them not, to come unto me: for of such is the kingdom of heaven.

Matthew 19:14 (KJV)

Oh, how I hated to go to the door to answer the insistent knock. The tub of tepid water in which I had just immersed myself was so soothing! I needed to relax, to wash away the grime and stickiness of a morning spent in the sun-hot garden and the steamy kitchen, picking and preparing tomatoes for canning. The fruits of my labors, a dozen jewel-red jars, gleamed brightly from the kitchen counter where they were cooling.

But the knock grew more demanding, and now it was accompanied by the ringing of the doorbell, loud enough that it would surely wake the baby. I was glad to have her settled for her nap and the other children happy on the playground.

Grabbing a towel and a robe, I left wet footprints on the

stairs as I hurried down. Just as I suspected. An unfavorite neighborhood urchin stood on the steps, still knocking as he saw my face appear at the window. Opening the door, I saw that he had two grimy cronies in tow. He wanted only a drink of water but made his parched request like a man dying on the Sahara. His blond-headed friend needed to telephone his mother (it sounded like a national emergency), and the one with freckles shifted nervously from one foot to the other as I unlocked the screen to let him fly to the bathroom. Sometimes I wondered at the so-called "convenience" of living next door to the playground!

I granted their requests, of course, but most ungraciously, full of exasperation that they had interfered with my well-deserved rest from labor. Yes, I could hear the baby shaking her crib. The slamming of the bathroom door had awakened her. My rest time, barely begun, was over. I shut the door harder than necessary when the last of the intruders straggled out. And the sound of the slamming woke me up too.

O Lord, I remember you said that if I had done it to the least of these I had done it to you. And it is true. If I am unloving toward one of these little ones, I cannot claim to love you who died for me. Forgive my stupid, selfish, hostile hates and all the unrecognized petty things about me. Make me anew in the image of God, serving all your creatures—especially the least of these—with love. AMEN.

Dog Days

God is our refuge and strength, a very present help in trouble.

Psalm 46:1 (KJV)

It was my morning off from work, so I took our four little ones and their friend Michael for a long walk down an unpaved street. Tommy wanted to show me a "rabbit bathtub" in the woods. It turned out to be a water fountain in the tree-lined front yard of a moneyed resident of the neighborhood. No rabbits were bathing just then, to the extreme disappointment of the younger children.

On our way back home we were startled by the yipping of a little white dog that came running out toward us. There'd have been no problem except that I was carrying baby Susan on my shoulders and Michael appeared to be quite frightened of the dog. He began to scream, the dog yipped louder, and Dino started yelling too. I couldn't reach either of the little boys to comfort them because Susan, squealing with delight, was bouncing up and down on my neck with decapitating enthusiasm. I couldn't have picked everyone up at once so I finally did the only practical thing. I set the baby down in the street and picked up the dog.

The woman who owned the panic-causing canine came out onto her porch just then to see what all the fuss was about. I apologized to her, gave her the dog, rescued Susan dripping from the mud puddle, and headed for home, halfway resolved not to invite Michael along the next time we went for a walk together.

When we were almost home, Michael stopped sniffling and pulled his shoulders back bravely.

"You know, I wasn't really afraid of that dog," he confided. "I was just pretending."

O my heavenly Father, how much trouble I cause sometimes because I am afraid, or worried, or unnecessarily upset about something. People have to go to all sorts of bother to console me, to make me feel secure again. Don't let me make their inconvenience unappreciated by acting as if I could have handled the situation all by myself. And don't let me act as if your grace is ever unnecessary. I ask in the holy name of Jesus who died that I might live. AMEN.

Enough and to Spare

And look out for each other's interests, not for your own interests.

Philippians 2:4 (TEV)

Rationing. Priorities. The words carry vivid memories for those who were old enough to be aware of some of the problems of everyday living during the Second World War. My father-in-law recollects his plight during those days when farming was complicated by the short supply of necessary equipment.

His patience was exhausted. For months he had been badgering the local ration board for a priority to buy a spare tire for his farm truck. Delay followed delay in what he supposed was just an endless ribbon of meaningless red tape.

Deciding to take the bull by the horns, he by-passed the "channels of appeal" and called upon the chairman of the local board, forcefully explaining his need, a need which

17

had grown more urgent with all his weeks of indignation about it.

Mr. B—— heard him through without comment but with a restrained smile. Then he explained:

"Mister, this thing is about to drive me crazy. I don't mean any disrespect or offense to you for I'm sure you just don't realize what you are asking—but anyhow, just as soon as I can arrange, *somehow,* to get a *fourth* tire for all these other people who are breathing fire down my neck," he paused to riffle through a thick pile of application papers, *"then* I'll do the best I can to get a fifth tire for you."

O Lord, forgive. How often I am impatient for luxuries while others about me lack bare necessities. I long for carpets while others have no floors but dirt. I yearn for wallpaper while many have no walls. Make me mindful of the urgent needs of others. Take away the selfishness that always thinks of my self and my comfort first. Make me so to love that I will be aware of the needs of others and able to share my substance with them, joyfully. I do ask in Jesus' holy name. AMEN.

Modern Improvements?

There is great gain in godliness with contentment; for we brought nothing into the world, and we cannot take anything out of the world; but if we have food and clothing, with these we shall be content. But those who desire to be rich fall into temptation, into a snare, into many senseless and hurtful desires that plunge men into ruin and destruction.

1 Timothy 6:6–9 (RSV)

Better is an handful with quietness, than both the hands full with travail and vexation of spirit.

Ecclesiastes 4:6 (KJV)

APOLOGIES TO PHYLLIS McGINLEY
(who wrote Nothing Ever Works for Me)

Oh, everything always works for me—
On ordinary days:
The sweeper sweeps, the drier dries,
And winsome are the children's ways,

19

And if, by chance, the coffeepot breaks,
I can fix it easy in a couple of shakes.
Oh, everything always works for me—
On ordinary days.

But let me plan a social spree
And ask some dinner company:
The vacuum bag bursts on the living room rug;
The kids fall into the hole they've dug;
The cooker lid soars like a ballistic missile,
Bombarding the ceiling with budget-beef gristle;
The milkman leaves me milk that's sour;
And life gets hecticker by the hour.

How do I stand it, what do I do
When hairpins won't fix, and neither will glue?
I phone my friends: "My regrets there be
For circumstances quite beyond me."
What of the rug and the kids and the ceiling?
From Scarlett I borrow:
"I'll think about them—
Tomorrow."

O Lord, some days it seems to me that modern inventions have made my life much too complicated. No wonder mamas take tranquilizers, babies have pacifiers, presidents have to sit in rocking chairs, and teenagers go delinquent. They don't have enough calming necessary tasks to do. Sweeping a floor with a broom was dusty business, but soothing somehow. Vacuuming to the tune of a steady roar isn't quite so restful. Washing dishes was tiring sometimes, but not nerve racking like having to retrieve shattered bits of crockery from under a grid in my automatic dishwasher. Scrubbing clothes on a washboard was strenuous exercise, but it did give a feeling of accomplishment. When my modern washing machine gets a baby sock floated overboard into the pump, and the linoleum is flooded clear to the dining room, and the repairman can't promise to come until the middle of next week, I see some advantage in the old dependable way of doing things. And when teenagers had to saw the logs for the fireplace and shell the peas for supper, they grew up more responsible automatically. Now we have to work at finding them constructive things to do.

Forgive me, Lord, that I become so easily unhinged. Let me be grateful for the labor-saving devices I have. Let me use the time they save to serve others for you. To do more constructive living. But let me be thankful and not striving after things that don't help. I do thank you. AMEN.

Who Knows?

A new commandment I give you: love one another. As I have
loved you, so you must love one another. If you have love for one
another, then all will know that you are my disciples.

John 13:34–35 (TEV)

The doctors said she was dying, and so she
seemed to be as she lay all agony there in her hospital bed.
But my hand placed on hers, and a simple prayer for God's
love to flow through her, stopped her writhing and let her
sigh for a moment in release and then rest. Her mouth
was so parched that what voice she had strength to use
was hard to understand. She was grateful for water and
orange juice dropped from a straw into her mouth. After
a while I did understand two words: "I hungry."

Borrowing some money from her roommate, I went
down to the snack shop and got some cream of chicken
soup warmed for her. Testing it against my wrist, as I

23

would test milk for a baby, I waited until I was sure it couldn't burn, then dripped its nourishment on her tongue as long as she welcomed it by opening her mouth, like a baby bird starving for its breakfast.

I went home soon, leaving her alone because the nurse asked me to go. There was nothing I could do, she said. And the woman wouldn't know whether I had been there or not.

So I left, believing that she *did* know I was there. That someone was there who loved her and wanted her to be whole.

That was Tuesday night. We buried her within a week.

O Father, who created us perfect and free, would my staying have made a difference? Would it have made a difference if every time she opened wide and staring eyes, frightened at surroundings that were not her home, there had been one there to hold her hand and assure her of your love, your care, your relief from pain? And to drip nourishment in her mouth?

The death certificate said she died of cancer. But did she really die of that? Or of our lack of faith in your healing love and power? Or of starvation for food and fellowship?

I am thankful she is with you now and doesn't suffer from our lack of attention. But give us who remain the grace to know your will and to do it, whether it seems foolish to others or not. In Jesus' name I ask it. AMEN.

24

Party Invitation

"Do not be worried and upset," Jesus told them.

John 14:1 (TEV)

My daughter Alice was not quite three years old when she was invited to Robbie's birthday party. She'd never been to a birthday party before.

I told her about the invitation and explained about the ice cream and cake, the balloons, the games they would play, and how much fun she'd have. To my surprise she didn't look happy at all, but started to cry, looking *quite* miserable.

"Why, what's wrong?" I asked. "You'll have such a good time—don't you want to go?"

She shook her head no, nearly sobbing now, and stammered, "Robbie will hit me!" She'd had some experience in playing with him before.

25

Dear Lord, I confess I had to laugh when Alice got so upset thinking about something bad that might never happen at all. But am I not the same way? How often I bemoan things that I should look forward to with exceeding joy. I anticipate troubles that never come and grieve over them. How foolish I am to plan a picnic and worry, "Oh dear, what if it rains?" Or to spoil a new dress by thinking, "It'll probably shrink when I wash it." Give me the grace to enjoy all good things without having to borrow trouble to spoil them. I do thank you. In Jesus' name. AMEN.

Wiggly Babies

Bless the Lord, O my soul; and all that is within me, bless his holy name! Bless the Lord, O my soul, and forget not all his benefits.

Psalm 103:1–2 (RSV)

My husband was trying to get Maria diapered and dressed while I finished my own share of the Sunday morning chores to get us all ready for Sunday school. Maria was being especially lively that morning, and the pins were more stubborn than usual about going through the diapers. It was enough to make my husband complain about how wiggly she was, how difficult to dress.

I was aware of the situation and wanted so much to offer some advice. "If you'd put her head through first, honey, and then do her arms one at a time, it wouldn't be nearly so hard as trying to do all three at once." I thought it, but didn't say it, because unsought advice is not his favorite dish—nor mine. We take different approaches to many things, including dressing babies. I was grateful to have his help and didn't want to spoil it.

O most gracious Lord, forgive me that I too have been a complainer about babies who wiggle and squirm while I try to get their shirts on or their shoes tied. You have caused me to remember Pat, a young woman who never wiggles when her parents dress her, when they tie the shoes that never stand on the floor, or when they put food into the mouth that cannot turn away.

Oh how merciful you have been to me, to give me a child that can move and resist movement. I do thank you and glorify your name. And I do pray for Pat and her parents that their loving patience may be rewarded with blessings above all they could ask or think. For your precious name's sake. AMEN.

Kittens—Cats

Each one must use the special gift he has received from God for the good of others, as a good manager of God's different gifts.

1 Peter 4:10 (TEV)

Where a man has been given much, much will be expected of him; and the more a man has had entrusted to him the more he will be required to repay.

Luke 12:48 (NEB)

The kids had called me to the screen door in a kind of cooperative chorus. Wondering why there was not at least one discordant note, I dried my hands and hurried to see what they wanted. One of them held a scrawny, mangy, obviously flea-bitten kitten up to my eye level.

"Mama, can we have it? It's for *free!*"

They had never heard, bless 'em, that sometimes they could earn money by offering to take a whole batch of kittens off someone's hands.

We were planning to leave for a week's vacation the next day, so, with that as an excuse, I talked them out of that particular feline. There were other opportunities later, however, and eventually we succumbed. Someone gave us two kittens—for free.

They were the dearest things, nice and cuddlesome, too little to jump on tables or do anything else that would have been destructive to our household. They didn't eat much either, at first, and one can of kitty food lasted for several days.

But soon it all changed. The kittens became cats, snagging nylons hanging on the line, significantly increasing our food bill—even when we used powdered skim milk for them—adding to our vacation expenditures as we had to pay for their room and board—and that of their current progeny—at the vets when we went away, and frustrating us all with their propensities for sneaking into the house whenever the kitchen door was opened, especially if there was company meat on the table. The day one climbed up under the hood of our neighbor's car and streaked out howling, minus his tail, when she started up to go to the grocery store, I had had enough.

Not only did I not want the cats, I didn't want to be responsible for their euthanasia either. I'd have gladly given someone—anyone—enough food to last 'em for a year and paid 'em ten dollars apiece to boot to take those cats off my hands.

O Father, your gift of salvation was costly to you, but free to me if I will accept it. But I can't just accept and forget. I have to give my life to keep it. And in giving my life, I find myself so showered with blessings that I know you are constantly serving me at continual cost to yourself. I thank you for it. Let me serve uncomplaining too. AMEN.

Obeying Rules

And Jesus said, "The Sabbath was made for the good of man; man was not made for the Sabbath."

Mark 2:27 (TEV)

I had a rather interesting run-in with the garbage-truck driver years ago. Our two garbage cans were full. So were a lot of extra boxes and buckets of bush trimmings, discarded glass jars, and other throwaways from spring housecleaning and general yard "ridding up" of the weekend.

I saw the man come into the yard and empty the contents of one can into his big container. Then he went out and dumped it in the truck, stopping to say something to the fat driver who, with much puffing and panting, got off his haunches and waddled into the back yard.

I went out to say hi and to tell him, as nicely as I could, which of the stuff was to go and which was to stay—the latter being only the empty garbage cans, the two buckets,

31

and a wastebasket. I wanted to keep the containers but was eager to be rid of their contents. Some of them were beginning to be malodorous. Finishing my polite instructions, I said thank you and turned back toward the house.

But the driver had a speech to make. He put his hands behind his back and delivered it.

"I'm sorry, lady, but we're only allowed to empty the stuff when it's in the big garbage can. We aren't supposed to empty wastebaskets or pick up boxes full of trash."

It was a good rule, undoubtedly effective in preventing garbage collectors from carting off something I might want to keep. But *surely* the rule could be temporarily set aside since I was there to make my wishes known? No, the driver insisted on adhering to the rule exactly.

So, with him watching, I picked up all the soaking stuff —it had been raining all morning—and filled the garbage cans with it as fast as the other man could empty them into his container and haul the trash to the truck. He made about five trips, with the driver just standing there, watching us work. Every once in a while he would make his speech again, never changing a word of it.

When I had finished putting the last of the debris into the garbage can for dumping into the big cardboard box and thence into the truck, I thanked the driver and went into the house. From my window I watched the last box load as the collector lifted it to his shoulder and carried it to the street. He was close to the truck when the rain-soaked bottom of the box gave way and a dozen or more glass jars smashed to the pavement.

I didn't know whether to laugh or to cry. Several other box carriers had arrived by that time, and they took shovels from the back of the truck and scooped *some* of the broken glass off the street. When the truck went on down the street, I got my broom and dustpan and went out to finish the street-sweeping job. It was about time for my husband to come home to lunch, and I didn't think the budget could stand a flat tire, especially with the prospect of hospital bills within the next few weeks when I was scheduled to go to the hospital for the birth of our fourth child.

O Lord, you know how indignant I was at the garbage-truck driver, that he could stand there letting his rules interfere with what common courtesy, an ounce of chivalry, and Christian love would have done for a woman very much "with child." But I am just as unbending, Lord, so often. I insist on my right of way when a few seconds of inconvenience could let another waiting driver turn left or enter the highway; or I insist that a tired child finish unimportant chores when I could help; or I insist that all work be finished before a child can play with a friend who has come to see her. How often I have let short-sighted rules of my own making delay God's kingdom! Forgive me any righteous indignation that is not directed at my own shortcomings. In Jesus' name. Amen.

A Healthy Sink Trap

Prove all things; hold fast that which is good.

1 Thessalonians 5:21 (KJV)

When our first baby was nine months old, it was necessary for me to go to work. I hired a young woman to come every day to take care of my baby and to keep the housework done so I'd have time for him when I came home at night. Tommy and Lucy loved each other, and I never worried that he'd be neglected in her care.

But sometimes I learned disquieting things. One evening as we were taking her home from work, I asked Lucy how she was getting along feeding Tommy regular food since he had graduated from puréed baby food. I explained that when she opened a can of string beans she could heat them with a little bacon grease for seasoning. Garden peas would be better with a pat of butter, and so on.

Lucy understood. "Oh, yes ma'am," she said. "I always

does that. I dumps out the water what's on 'em awready and puts on new water and cooks 'em with butter."

O Lord, you know the dismay I felt when I thought of our healthy, vitamin-enriched sink trap and my poor, vitamin-deprived child. And what pains I took to explain to Lucy that she must never throw away the nutritious liquid in the can or substitute water for it! But don't I do the same thing day after day? Don't I cast away what should be the most spiritually nourishing part of life, thinking I can replace it with something better? Don't I neglect study of your Word for unimportant busyness? Don't I rush about in fruitless action when it would be better to pray? Do stop me and teach me where the better part lies, that I may partake of it and feed it to my children, for your name's sake. AMEN.

Automatic Me

We ought, therefore, to pay the greatest attention to the truth
that we have heard and not allow ourselves to drift away from it.

Hebrews 2:1 (Phillips)

It was Saturday morning, and I was on my
way to the grocery store to replenish the refrigerator and
cupboard so we'd have something to eat in the week that
lay ahead. My eleven-year-old son was along; I had to take
him to the hospital for his allergy shot. Combining the two
trips made sense because of the location of the hospital near
the grocery store.

We were busy talking as I approached the intersection
where I needed to go straight ahead instead of turning left
as I ordinarily did when I was going only to the store.
Without thinking, I signaled for my left turn and was
halfway down the block before I realized my mistake.
James was not at all surprised. "Oh, that's all right, Mom,"
he explained. "Everybody's automatic nowadays."

I had shuddered at the thought of machines taking over the world. I had been disgusted time after time when inquiries that could not be answered by a standard form letter drew only nonanswering form letters in reply. And I had been outraged when second notices for bills, and even very indignant third notices, were spat out from a machine and mailed to me long after a personal representative of the company had acknowledged my payment, my canceled subscription, my returned merchandise or what have you. And now I had joined them. I had just learned from my son that in an automatic world, people had become automatic too.

It was bad enough that machines could do many things better than I could. But that I had become an automaton, performing in an automatic, nonthinking way when it didn't suit my purposes—well, it was as bad—almost—as the day I turned forty.

O Father, forgive that I so automatically accept all your blessings that I fail to notice the turnings where you are beckoning me to go an unaccustomed way. Root out of me any habits that lead me astray from your purpose and will for my life. Let me truly pay attention to you and not lose your truth—automatically. In Jesus' name I pray. Amen.

A Striking Resemblance

Do not think of yourselves more highly than you should. Instead, be modest in your thinking.

Romans 12:3 (TEV)

It was fall, county fair time. We splurged and took Tommy and Alice to ride the merry-go-round, to drive the little cars, and chug merrily along in the choo-choo train. They got thoroughly initiated in cotton candy, sticky from ear to ear, and exclaimed in awe and admiration at the display of fireworks. We were on our way back to the car when we detoured to show them the livestock exhibits.

Tired from all the activity, both children were relatively subdued, dragging along, until suddenly Alice jerked her hand away from mine and darted up to a fence where she squealed with delight!

"Oh, Mama, that big pig looks just like me!" Her tone

was both surprised and impressed, as if it was a truly remarkable achievement for a little girl to look like a blue-ribbon pink pig at the county fair. The pig gave a low grunt at the little girl peering at him, as if the notion was somehow acceptable to him, too.

O Lord, what joy little children have! I'd be embarrassed to think that a pig looked like me and would certainly never voice such an opinion. Free me from misguided pompous notions and let me delight in all your creation as my child does. And make me humble enough to recognize that being an honest pig is preferable to being me when I'm trying to be what I'm not. I do thank you. AMEN.

Following the Recipe

Jesus answered them, 'Have faith in God. I tell you this: if anyone says to this mountain, "Be lifted from your place and hurled
into the sea," and has no inward doubts, but believes that what
he says is happening, it will be done for him. I tell you, then,
whatever you ask for in prayer, believe that you have received it
and it will be yours.'

Mark 11:22–24 (NEB)

Pray without ceasing.

1 Thessalonians 5:17 (KJV)

The effectual fervent prayer of a righteous man availeth much.

James 5:16 (KJV)

But when you pray, go into your room and shut the door and pray
to your Father who is in secret; and your Father who sees in secret
will reward you. And in praying do not heap up empty phrases
as the Gentiles do.

Matthew 6:6–7 (RSV)

41

Whenever two of you on earth agree about anything you pray for, it will be done for you by my Father in heaven. For where two or three come together in my name, I am there with them.

Matthew 18:19–20 (TEV)

Do not substitute! How often I've read, and heeded, that admonition in recipe books. When I've not heeded it, I've found out why it was so important. Recipes improperly followed, or carelessly, flagrantly deviated from, just don't bring the same results as careful measurements and letter-perfect adherence to the instructions. I understand my flops in cooking when I don't follow the recipe.

But how prone I am to think that prayer doesn't work, when I've not consulted the recipe at all, much less pretended to follow it.

For instance?

"Pray without ceasing," the Bible tells me. But I seldom do. I pray intermittently, or not at all. Why, I wouldn't dream of trying to bake a cake on the installment plan, in an intermittent oven. I wouldn't think of expecting it to be high and light, a delicious concoction to match the picture in the book, if I turned the oven off and on, baking as interruptedly as I pray.

"The effectual *fervent* prayer of a righteous man availeth much," James tells us. And how fervent am I? Quickie devotionals may include a hurried, post-amen intercession: "Oh, yes! P.S. Bless so and so. Amen." Fervent? Not hardly. About like trying to bake a hot-oven soufflé at a cool two hundred degrees. No wonder my prayers fall so flat sometimes.

Prayers of a righteous man? Even when God graciously counts my feeble faith as righteousness without my having lifted a finger in obedience, I fail to measure up to a reasonable standard.

"Suppose prayer doesn't work?" I ask myself. And, after I have prayed, giving a problem into my Lord's keeping, I think I have to keep checking on it myself. It's as if I tried to bake a beautiful cake, only instead of trusting the batter to the oven, took the cake out to check on it every three minutes, to stir up the beginning-to-bake batter, and start it over again, never believing it would turn out right. How could it—faced with the interference of my unbelief?

And two of us agreeing about anything we pray for? Aren't we more likely to argue? One wants to pray for the complete wholeness of a sick man. Another thinks it appropriate to pray only for his soul's salvation.

And when do I pray in secret? And when do I refrain from piling up hollow words and empty phrases while my heart is somewhere else?

O God, forgive me that I've ever thought prayer didn't "work." I hadn't even read the recipe, much less assembled the proper ingredients in the right order, turned on the oven and prepared to follow the directions. Lord, if it isn't too late, if I'm not too obtuse, Lord, teach me to pray! AMEN.

Remembering Christmas

I have come in order that they might have life, life in all its fulness.

John 10:10 (TEV)

Whatever you do, put your whole heart and soul into it, as into work done for God, and not merely for men.

Colossians 3:23 (Phillips)

We had gone to visit a friend who lived in a little house in a very unprosperous section of town. It was a week before Christmas, and her house was in the full bloom of celebration! There was a scraggly tree in the living room, laden with homemade decorations. A wreath, rescued from last year's junk heap, hung on the front door. Christmas cards made a bright parade on the mantel, and a little manger scene on a low table beckoned our devotion.

I was ashamed to think that I hadn't put up a tree yet. And my door was still undecorated. Worse yet, our manger scene was packed away in the attic!

45

One of the kids said it for me when we got back in the car to head for home:

"Mama, Virginia might not have much, but she sure remembers Christmas with all she's got!"

"Living within your means—" I had always emphasized the last part of the expression, the limiting part, but I woke up that day. It's the first part that should have the emphasis. What I was planning to do in the way of Christmas decoration *was* within my means, of course, within the budget of time and money I had allotted for our celebration. But whether you could call it *living* or not, by the remotest stretch of a charitable imagination, was another thing entirely.

O Lord, forgive! No wonder the picture of Jesus that hangs on the wall over the piano has fallen to the floor every day for the past week! Is it just that the wall is damp, and the tape old and unsticky? Perhaps, but maybe not. Maybe you've been trying to get my attention—to wake me up to notice you. And to bless me as I remember.

A birthday is coming—make me to celebrate it with everything I've got—and to acknowledge that everything I've got came from you—and belongs to you still. AMEN.

Fuzzy Thinking

You don't have to read between the lines of my letters; you can understand them.

2 *Corinthians* 1:13 (Moffatt)

THAT THINKING FEELING

> I lack the knack of
>   ambiguity—
>
> wouldn't have it
>   as a gift,
>
> except on days my
>   perspicuity
>
> bares the fact
>   my mind's adrift.

O Lord, you know I like to be plainspoken so that people can understand me. But sometimes, when I've been com-

47

pletely wrong, I wish I had been a little less clear. Then I could hide behind fuzzy words and say, "Well, you didn't understand what I meant," and so appear to be in the right always. Take this foolish pride away from me. Let me always want to speak out boldly, witnessing to the things I have seen and heard. For how else will I ever learn my errors, unless I am plain enough for men to understand and correct me? I thank you for this grace and for all others. In Jesus' name. AMEN.

Woman's Place

> Then the Lord God said, "It is not good that the man should be
> alone; I will make him a helper fit for him."
>
> *Genesis 2:18* (RSV)

I was surprised to see my husband driving up
in our neighbor's car to bring me home from the hospital
with our third baby. He explained that in the press of
things he had put three-year-old Tommy in the car to wait
for him while he took care of a few last-minute things in
the house. The few last-minute things stretched into half
an hour or so because the sitter who was to stay with our
fifteen-monther was late in arriving.

The delay was long enough that Tommy had the bat-
tery completely useless by the time Allen got to the car.
And so he had borrowed our neighbor's.

Several other memorable things happened at home
while I was in the hospital. Some of the highlights came to
my attention in the weeks that followed:

The peculiar smell in the kitchen was kerosene that had

seeped under the refrigerator, cabinets, washing machine, etc. The floor furnace had gone out during the night, and Allen had to soak up the flooded oil with a sponge and squeeze it into a pan before he dared to relight the fire. The pan was on the floor and so was the fifteen-monther. No permanent damage.

The new glass top on the hydrator in the refrigerator was necessitated by a hot pan of hot soup being set on the old one to cool.

The gray look on everything in the living room was a reminder that one day Allen had borrowed a vacuum cleaner to get things spruced-up for my return. The vacuuming done, he went to another part of the house to get dressed to return it. Tommy had stayed with the vacuum cleaner which he had enjoyed—so much that by the time my husband got back to the living room, Tommy had opened the cleaner and sprinkled little piles of dirt all over the rug, sofa, chairs, and tables so he could watch the cleaning operation once more.

"Sweep it again, Daddy."

O Lord, I am so thankful that you did not make man to live alone but to need a helpmate to keep his home in reasonable order. I thank you that you did plan for families and made me a necessary part of one. I thank you that there are many things my husband does better than I do and that you, in your great wisdom and mercy, have given us traits that complement one another. I thank you that you have created us male and female, have given us a house to keep, children to raise, and one another to cherish. And most of all I thank you for your son to save me. In Jesus' name. AMEN.

Lost in the Woods

I have gone astray like a lost sheep.

Psalm 119:176 (KJV)

I will instruct you and teach you the way you should go; I will counsel you with my eye upon you.

Psalm 32:8 (RSV)

I must have been nearly eight years old when my two younger brothers and I went to the woods on our ten-acre farm to hunt bears. We thought we *probably* wouldn't see a bear, but were well-armed, just in case, with guns made of matchsticks thrust through the center of empty sewing-thread spools. Sturdy rubber bands provided our firing power. Well-equipped, we crossed the field where Bossy, our only cow, was tied to a stake so she could graze on the green grass. Bessie, our only pig, rooted happily in a fenced enclosure nearby.

Being in the woods was fun, for a while, and the three of us felt quite adventuresome stalking through the bushes.

But I became frightened in a little while when a cloud obscured the sun and the awful cobwebs brushed at me from every direction. We were lost—afraid that we might see a bear after all—and that, worse still, he might see us.

I had started to cry about the cobwebs, but Don, two years younger than I, wasn't about to show that he was afraid. He climbed a tree to see if he could find the way out of the woods. It was easy. When he had climbed above the level of the brush and bushes, he could see the cow, still grazing. And if we had stopped to listen, we could have heard fat Bessie's contented grunts.

O Lord, how lost and frightened and far from home I can feel myself to be. Teach me, instead of vainly striving to find my way out of my lostness, to climb up, to reach up, to stretch up above the cobwebs of despair clutching at me, to see that you are very near always, and that seeking I may find you. I ask in Jesus' name. AMEN.

Washing Instructions

Wash yourselves; make yourselves clean; remove the evil of your doings from before my eyes; cease to do evil, learn to do good; seek justice, correct oppression; defend the fatherless, plead for the widow.

Isaiah 1:16–17 (rsv)

Though your sins be as scarlet, they shall be as white as snow; though they be red like crimson, they shall be as wool.

Isaiah 1:18 (kjv)

It was Susan's fifth birthday. Inside the pretty package she received in the mail that day was a lovely pink terry bathrobe from her Ohio grandmama. As she tried it on, Susan hugged herself up in it and handed me a laundry instruction ticket from the pocket.

"Here, Mama," she said. "It says when it gets dirty you're supposed to wash it!"

I laughed aloud at the obviousness of the instructions.

Of course I'd wash it when it got dirty. Didn't I always wash clothes when they became soiled?

O Lord, forgive me that what is so obvious to me about washing soiled clothing is so often neglected in my spiritual welfare. My soul needs frequent cleansing too, to restore its purity. Only that isn't a do-it-myself job. I have to invite you to do it for me. And I'm so reluctant sometimes. As if I'd rather stay dirty than be made clean by your grace. I am ashamed to ask it so often, ashamed not to take better care of what you have made clean at such great cost. For Jesus' sake, keep me in the right way, that I will not get muddied again so soon. Let me feel the cost of your sacrifice and not lightly make it necessary time after time. Let me live in the full realization that you don't just take my sins and dump them somewhere, but you have to bear them yourself. Let me not add to the weight of them. I thank you. AMEN.

*T*ruth and *C*onsequences

You will know the truth, and the truth will make you free.

John 8:32 (TEV)

Once upon a time I was an alleged teacher of a class of first graders in the Sunday school program of our church. One night, all primary teachers were required to attend a committee meeting to discuss "The Nature of Primary Children."

There was a cub scout meeting going on in the building the same evening. And our committee chairman was acutely aware of the hordes of scouts tromping up and down the hallway outside the classroom where we were meeting.

There, I thought, *that racket provides a good, realistic background for a meeting of this sort.* I had been having some discipline problems with one of my little pupils. And tired as I was, having rushed home from work to prepare

55

supper for my family and dash to the meeting, I settled back to listen to our chairman and to learn how to cope with the nature of primary children from 9:45–10:45 every Sunday morning.

Do you suppose that's what we discussed? Not on your life! The chairman, who had no children of her own, slammed the door angrily against the disturbance outside, and proceeded to rhapsodize about the endearing qualities of six-year-olds. The discussion was a shade unrealistic, to say the least, even though we had been made to sit in the tiny ten-inch-high chairs our primary children used, in order better to "identify" with the subject of the discussion. I must confess that my mind kept straying to the bedlam in the hallway, which was probably but a faint echo of the bedlam occurring in my house where I had left my own little ones with an expensive baby-sitter so I could go to the committee meeting to learn about their nature.

O Lord, how unrealistic we can get! When the facts don't fit our program, we usually ignore the facts, pretending they don't exist. But didn't you say that it was truth that would make us free? I want to be free, Lord. So give me to know what I know, to impart what I know, and not to stand for artificiality in committees or anywhere else. Let your truth lead me. I ask in Jesus' holy name. AMEN.

Feeling Faint

Even the youths shall faint and be weary, and the young men shall utterly fall.

Isaiah 40:30 (KJV)

To him who is able to keep you from falling, and present you faultless and joyful before his glory—to the only God our Savior, through Jesus Christ our Lord, be glory, majesty, might, and authority, from all ages past, and now, and for ever and ever! Amen.

Jude 24–25 (TEV)

Tommy had broken his collarbone and was spending a few days in the hospital. His release was postponed when he developed a bad case of tonsillitis. The doctors didn't want to let him go home until his temperature had returned to normal.

Impatient from the beginning, eager to get back to school to show off his cast, Tommy teased to be allowed to get out of bed. One afternoon he made up his mind to walk to the bathroom. Sure of his own strength, he shrugged my hand away when I reached out to support him.

"Do you think you can make it alone?" I asked.

He nodded, *almost* vigorously. "You don't need to help me," he said. "I can do it by myself."

But I was glad I had stayed nearby. As he slid from the edge of the bed to stand on his own two feet, his eyes grew puzzled. He took one tentative step away from the bed, and then another. When he began to sway, his voice wavered too.

"I don't feel like myself—" he said, as his knees buckled under him. He didn't protest as I caught him and helped him back to bed.

O Lord, how many times I have known, "I don't feel like myself," when I've tried to do something without inviting or permitting you to help me. Forgive me my stubborn independent streaks. Make me ever to know that "Thou hast made us for Thyself" and I cannot be my true self until I let you keep me from falling. In Jesus' holy name. AMEN.

Ignorance, Bliss?

But if any man be ignorant, let him be ignorant.

1 Corinthians 14:38 (KJV)

After all, who are you to criticize the servant of somebody else, especially when that somebody else is God? It is to his own master that he gives, or fails to give, satisfactory service.

Romans 14:4 (Phillips)

One hot summer morning of my childhood I awoke to an unmistakable aroma in the air. I didn't have to look out my bedroom window to know that our hired man was spreading stable manure on the cornfield behind the house. It wouldn't have concerned me ordinarily, but the breeze was blowing in the worst possible direction, and I had invited a rather sophisticated city friend to spend the day with me.

Making the best of an awful situation, I rehearsed some elaborate apologies, but they were not needed. When my friend arrived she stepped from the car, wrinkled her nose with obvious pleasure, and took a deep, deep breath, exclaiming, "That's what I love about the country, the smell of new-mown hay!"

I almost spoiled it by telling her which season was for harvesting and which for planting, but fortunately I caught myself in time. We had a fine day, with her ecstasy over new-mown hay and my ecstasy over her ignorance.

O Lord, deliver me from the sinfulness of a life full of apologies, either spoken or felt as inward cringings. If I stop judging, then I will stop apologizing for others. Don't let me be like the wives who interrupt when their husbands begin to tell a story they've heard too many times already. The other listeners may enjoy it. And don't let me be overly apologetic about things I do. Let me do as well as I am able and present the results before you humbly, serving you according to the ability you have planted in me. Let me waste no precious energy in planning apologies for things that will please others after all. Let me live honestly. In Jesus' name I ask it. AMEN.

Morning Glory

Very early the next morning, long before daylight, Jesus got up and left the house. He went out of town to a lonely place where he prayed.

Mark 1:35 (TEV)

The steadfast love of the Lord never ceases, his mercies never come to an end; they are new every morning.

Lamentations 3:22–23 (RSV)

He has made everything beautiful in its time.

Ecclesiastes 3:11 (RSV)

I was up early and outside hanging up the day's laundry. The grass and trees, damp with dew, had a veritable glow of greenness about them. And the birds were still shrieking raucously, heralding the morning sun. The sky was so blue it hurt my eyes to look at it, and there were freshly white billows of clouds spread out to dry. Such beauty there was—and how seldom I got outside early enough to notice it.

Another morning I was up earlier still. And as I looked out the windows toward the east, I was thrilled to see the sun rise. A tall pine, silhouetted blackly against the reddening sky, made me think of the other sunrises I had seen —in technicolor, in movies about African safaris.

O Father, forgive me that I so ignore the beauty you have created for me that I have seen more movies of African safaris than I have seen sunrises in my own backyard. How full of praise and rejoicing Jesus must have been as he went out early to pray in the midst of your dawning creation. Teach me to go outdoors to pray too, where I can be aware of the sparrows and the lilies of the field instead of the bills to be paid, the floors to be swept, and the ironing to be done. Fill me to overflowing with the beauty of your creation so that I may truly see "how great Thou art" and reverently worship you in all that I do. In Jesus' name. Amen.

Beautiful upon the Mountain? Not Mine!

For it is by God's grace that you have been saved, through faith. It is not your own doing, but God's gift. There is nothing here to boast of, since it is not the result of your own efforts.

Ephesians 2:8–9 (TEV)

I've always had the kind of humility that could stoop to wash another's feet. Mamas get used to doing that kind of service. But to let another wash mine? And see all the thickened broken toenails, all the ugly peeling skin, touch all the scratchy corns and deep-ribbed callouses, inhale all the aromas of shoes long worn?

Mercy!

If I belonged to a footwashing church, as some of my friends do, I'd go wearing brand-new shoes—whether I needed them and could afford them or not—well sprinkled with deodorant powder. My feet and stockings would be as clean as soap and scrubbing and maybe a little bleach could make them. How could I disguise their ugliness? I'd want to make it seem that my feet had never been dirty or smelly, that I'd never worn heels too high and shoes too tight and spoiled the feet God gave me.

O Lord, that's how I do before Christ too. You invite me to come just as I am because it is only you who can effect a change in me, who can make me new again. But I want to take care of all my sinnings first, all my defects and blemishes, before I open the door where you've been so patiently knocking forever. I want to join you, possessing already a goodness that can come only from being with you.

Forgive my pride. Forgive me that I want to think I have cleansed myself, by myself, or pretend that I have never been stained by sin. Help me to know that although I can wash my own feet I can never wash away my sin. And if I am able, one day, to be presented faultless before my maker, it will be because Jesus died to cleanse me. Don't let me forget. In Jesus' name. AMEN.

Alias

The man who goes in by the door is the shepherd of the sheep. The gatekeeper opens the gate for him; the sheep hear his voice as he calls his own sheep by name, and he leads them out.

John 10:2–3 (TEV)

Our Tommy was enrolled in Vacation Bible School at the church. One day I arrived early to pick him up so he was not out on the sidewalk waiting for me. Going inside, I told the woman in charge that I was Tommy Harrell's mother, and I would just sit down and wait until his class was dismissed. She looked rather mystified, but didn't say anything until she had read over her class charts to make sure she was right.

"I'm sorry," she said. "You must be at the wrong place. We don't have any Tommy Harrell enrolled here."

Now I was the mystified one. I asked for permission to look into the classroom. I saw Tommy at once, sitting at a small table, coloring a picture, and pointed him out to the woman.

"There he is," I said. "The little boy in the blue shirt."

She shook her head. "We have him down as Georgie," she explained, "Georgie Russell. And that's the name he has put on all his papers."

I understood then. We had let Tommy see a movie about Davy Crockett. One of the characters was Georgie Russell. And Tommy had pretended to be Georgie ever since.

O Lord, who am I? Do I pretend to be someone else? Are there days when my own mother wouldn't know me because of some foreign nature I put on myself like a mantle? Don't let me forget who I am, whose I am. Let me answer when you call me by name. For Jesus' sake. AMEN.

Night Out

Anyone who starts to plow and then keeps looking back is of no use for the Kingdom of God.

Luke 9:62 (TEV)

It is the one who has endured to the end who will be saved.

Mark 13:13 (NAS)

Dinner and party invitations were rare in those days, so I was thrilled when my husband's cousin and his wife invited us to come to Chapel Hill for supper. Afterward we were to attend a gala party together. I hired a baby-sitter for our three little ones for the evening, someone who'd helped me out a few times before, and pressed my still-almost-presentable best dress.

Leaving the sitter with all the necessary instructions about the supper and bedtime habits of our babies, we set off for the ninety-minute drive to the home of our host. When we arrived, his phone was ringing. It was for us.

67

The baby-sitter had decided that we should have a quick supper, skip the party, and return home as soon as possible. The children were proving too much for her.

Heartbroken at having our evening spoiled, I asked her to find someone to help her out with the children, and I would pay them, too. I told her the names of several sitters who might be available and suggested that I call her after supper to see if things were going well. We decided to have an ordinary supper in a nearby restaurant rather than go to Durham to the special place where our host had reservations.

After a hurried supper I called home again, learned that the children were all bathed and in bed, sleeping. Heaving a sigh of relief, I said, "Well, then, it's all right if we go to the party, isn't it."

"No," I was informed in no uncertain terms. "You'll have to come home right away."

No argument would dissuade her, and after several fruitless long-distance attempts to locate someone to take her place, we bade our friends goodbye and headed for home, our festive spirits flattened like an unsuccessful soufflé.

Forgive me, Lord, for the times when I've accepted jobs and then quit, for reasons no one could understand; for the times when my lack of foresight has inconvenienced someone who was counting on me. And now, these many years later, let me forgive that baby-sitter who wouldn't stay. I ask in Jesus' name. AMEN.

If the Shoe Doesn't Fit

For all the people of Athens and the foreigners who lived there liked to spend all their time telling and hearing the latest new thing.

Acts 17:21 (TEV)

       Alice had been complaining practically forever that her Sunday shoes were too small. When she wasn't being vocal about it, I kept being reminded anyway by the almost club-footed way she walked on Sunday mornings, keeping her toes curled up so her shoes wouldn't pop off her feet.

I finally got around to taking her to the shoe department of a store where we have a charge account. The clerk measured her foot, put new shoes on her, and Alice walked back and forth across the carpet a few times, pronouncing the shoes satisfactory. She was anxious to get back home to finish playing a basketball tournament.

I didn't pay too much attention. I didn't even feel to see if there was a thumb's space between the tip of her big toe and the end of her shoe. After all, she was thirteen years old and bright to boot—certainly old enough to know if a shoe fit or not.

Sunday morning came, and time to don the new footwear. Alice got dressed and—you guessed it—complained that her new shoes were already too tight. They seemed even worse than her old ones, she thought.

"Nonsense," I told her. "It's just because they're new. They'll be all right."

But her face continued to look sincerely and excruciatingly pained.

"Oh, well," I said. "Wear your old ones today if you think they'll feel better."

Her sigh of relief as she worked the new shoes off her feet made me wonder.

"Here, let me see one of your new shoes a minute," I said. "And one of your old ones, too, please."

You guessed it again. Matched heel and toe, the new shoes were a full size-and-a-half shorter than the old ones had been.

Forgive me, Lord, for the times I have foolishly thought that something new was automatically better than something old, that something new would give me rest when actually it proved to be more unsatisfactory than what I had before. Make me to give thanks in all things, that I may learn how to choose wisely what is best for me. I thank you, Father. AMEN.

70

Early Bird

And you, too, be ready, because the Son of Man will come at an hour when you are not expecting him.

Luke 12:40 (TEV)

One night, as we were finishing supper, the phone rang. The caller was an insurance adjuster checking to see if my lawyer husband was at home. He wanted to come to give him some checks to settle a case. When I gave him directions to our house, he said he would be there in about ten minutes. My husband got up from the table, to go back to the bedroom to change into his "lawyer suit." He had been outside working in the yard and looked a little more like a dirt farmer than a professional man. As he went, he explained that he'd get ready and meet the insurance man outside. They could transact their business in the car so there'd be no need for me to scramble the debris in the living room back the hallway to whatever

71

bedroom wasn't already overflowing with the evidence of a lived-in-look, never difficult to achieve in our crowded household of little ones.

I took him at his word, just as he had taken the insurance man at his, relaxed, and sat back down to continue feeding the baby her apricots. Allen took off his out-at-the-elbows corduroy shirt and his grimy khakis, tossed them on the davenport, and headed for the bedroom.

Someone was knocking at the door. I knew it couldn't be the insurance man already, probably just the paper boy wanting to collect thirty cents for last week. So I went to the door, kicking a path among the toys as I went, lugging my apricotty baby on one hip. I had the inevitable apricots and chicken-with-vegetables on *my* shirt too.

You know what I saw when I opened the door. No dungareed neighborhood kid but a properly necktied and starch-shirted insurance man. He apologized for arriving so soon. He hadn't realized, he said, that the phone from which he was calling was actually just down the street from our house. I smiled (I think) and invited him in. If he didn't trip on something maybe he wouldn't notice the mess.

Just then Allen came back down the hallway, barefoot, looking for some socks. He was in his undershirt—holey, like they'd all been for months. I was thankful he *had* put his trousers on.

I expected the man to turn and run, but he didn't. Seems he had four children of his own and understood the situation at least moderately well. I had been afraid he wouldn't trust Allen with the money, but he did.

O Lord, how often I think I can postpone or avoid getting ready for something that is just around the corner. And then, before I know it, it is upon me. Don't let me be like the foolish virgins whose lamps were without oil when the bridegroom came. Let me have my house in order for your coming. I ask in Jesus' name. AMEN.

*I*dle *I*dols

You shall have no other gods before me. You shall not make for yourself a graven image, . . . you shall not bow down to them or serve them.

Exodus 20:3–5 (RSV)

We know that an idol is nothing in the world, and that there is none other God but one.

1 Corinthians 8:4 (KJV)

"Jesus calls us . . . from each idol—" The line of the hymn had always conjured up a vision of a totem pole to me. And I had felt happily immune to the attraction of worshiping an idol like *that*. Not until God led me to realize what idols *were* keeping me from his service did I see what the hymn really meant. The idols I was worshiping were every bit as unworthy of worship as a painted stick: a clean house, the right paint for the wood-work, a measure of material success, and a good reputation

75

among my fellows were not bad aims, but they were quite unworthy of a lifetime's devotion.

Father, on this fortieth birthday forgive me that I have spent so much of my life in pursuing, yes, in giving worshipful devotion to, insignificant things. Let me acknowledge, by your grace, that you are actually calling me away from these things into total service to you. And instead of thinking of giving a little part of my money to your church, a portion of my time to your cause, a fraction of my talent to witnessing for you, to glorifying your name—let me think in terms not of giving, for all is already yours, but in terms of living, not my, but your whole life for you. For I belong to you. I thank you for showing me how life can begin at forty. Thank you for making me to look in the mirror and see what a nothing I am when I am not in you. Thank you for letting me know whose life I have been talking about. Let your life begin in me. This moment. AMEN.

Housecleaning

His blood will make our consciences clean from useless works, so that we may serve the living God.

Hebrews 9:14 (TEV)

Behold, I have refined you, but not like silver; I have tried you in the furnace of affliction.

Isaiah 48:10 (RSV)

It's funny how we measure progress sometimes—not by an accumulation of things to keep but by the heap of things to be thrown out. When I've spent a day housecleaning, I feel I've accomplished a great deal if I have a tremendous pile of junk for the trashman to cart away.

The windows may not be washed, the curtains may hang still dingy and limp, the floors and woodwork may be something less than sparkling clean, but if I've sorted out some of the cumbersome debris of living, I know I've

77

made progress. Cleaning's easier with some of the junk out of the way.

O Lord, teach me the spiritual truth of all I've learned. Do I need to neaten up my life, casting away all the superfluous dust-catchers that do not add to its beauty or its usefulness? Will it be easier, then, for me to see where the dirt lies, where the sins lurk, so that I might invite you to cleanse me from top to toe? I would be refined, and have the dross burnt away, that I might be wholly yours, sparkling in service for you. For your glory. AMEN.

Mouth Exter-size

O come, let us sing to the Lord; let us make a joyful noise to the rock of our salvation! Let us come into his presence with thanksgiving; let us make a joyful noise to him with songs of praise!

Psalm 95:1–2 (RSV)

Tommy was nine when he encountered a worrisome time conflict in his expanding activities. His baseball team had a big game scheduled for the very afternoon when he was supposed to go to church for choir practice. We discussed divided loyalties—mine, not his. His loyalty to a baseball team was in a far higher league than loyalty to any choir. Tommy concluded his pleadings and arguments with a sincere clincher:

"Besides, Mom, in baseball I get more mouth exter-size!"

Remembering the din of the chattering and cheering from the game the day before—the playground adjoined our backyard—I couldn't disagree about that.

O Father, don't I too get more mouth exercise in complaining, in ragging the opposition, in cheering my own team than I do in making a joyful noise unto the Lord? O Lord, so give me to live the life you have granted me that singing your praise will exercise not only my mouth but my spirit as well. Let seeking after you exercise my whole self more than seeking after any other thing. I thank you. In Jesus' name. AMEN.

On Not Thinking About It

Finally, brethren, whatever is true, whatever is honorable, whatever is just, whatever is pure, whatever is lovely, whatever is gracious, if there is any excellence, if there is anything worthy of praise, think about these things.

Philippians 4:8 (RSV)

SLAMMM!

That did it! The deliberate banging of the screen door behind my teenage son as he left the house for his scout meeting was the last straw. I clenched my fists, gritted my teeth, and took some long strides toward the door, intending to call him back for a real tongue-lashing. All day he'd gone out of his way to aggravate me, and had been extremely successful at getting my goat—but good. If his father had been at home, I'd have certainly called for a good paddling.

Fortunately for both of us, the telephone rang before I

reached the door. By the time my caller had finished her message, Tommy was long since out of sight and earshot. My harangue would have to wait until he got home.

In the meantime, I busied myself with bathing the baby and getting her ready for bed, unburdening myself to my younger son as I worked, complaining about all of Tommy's manifold transgressions. James listened, without saying much.

Then I went upstairs to tuck the baby into her crib for the night. It didn't take long, and when I came back downstairs I found my younger son still deep in thought.

"I think I know what would help you about Tommy, Mama," he said.

"You do, James? What is it?" At my rope's end, I was willing to listen to all suggestions even though I doubted that a mere child could come up with a hopeful solution to a relationship as broken as the one which existed, to my sorrow, between my son and myself. "What is it?" I asked.

"Well," he said simply, "just don't think about it."

I had to laugh out loud then, and chuckled the rest of the evening thinking about the utter inanity of what he had suggested. *As if my not thinking about a problem could possibly make it vanish, or diminish it in any way. The very idea!* It was dear of James to be concerned enough to suggest something, I thought, even if his suggestion wasn't helpful.

But the suggestion worked in my mind as I continued my chores. And the truth of it took possession of me. I wondered how many of my problems had magnified themselves all out of proportion by my dwelling on them inordinately. Plenty, I guessed.

And so, instead of thinking about my problems with

this particular child, about his apparent shortcomings, I turned my thoughts to God, to a contemplation of that loveliness with which he so abundantly fills my senses in the springtime, to his great mercy, which delights in forgiving all my wrongdoing, all my sins.

My child didn't become a paragon of virtue overnight, of course. Neither did I. But when, with my own soul flooded with the love of God, I treated my child like a child instead of a problem, he responded. Home from his meeting, his shoulders defensively braced against the prolonged scolding he expected, he headed glumly upstairs to bed. He looked startled when I said, "Tom, it *is* past your bedtime, I know, but the other kids had Pepsi floats tonight. Wouldn't you like to fix one for yourself before you turn in?" The surprise on his face almost covered the pleasure on it. When had I been merciful and loving to him? Could it have been so long?

Strangely, there was no mess left for me to clean up when he finished his refreshment. He washed his glass and spoon and returned them to the cupboard. That was unheard of! And he mumbled—still almost unbelieving, "Thanks, Mom," as he went to bed a few minutes later. The next morning, when I went in his room to wake him early so he could finish the homework he'd dawdled over the previous afternoon, I found him lying in bed smiling. He was propped up on one elbow with his speller and notebook open beside him.

"I'm already on the last sentence, Mom," he announced proudly.

O Father, forgive me again. Forgive me that I have read your word but have not had the sense to apply it to

83

my own life, to bless the lives of those about me, to strengthen in loveliness your children who live in this house. Have they had to bear burdens of imperfection so that you could teach me to love the unlovely? Have they been like princes imprisoned in toads until I could learn lessons necessary for my salvation? Has it been that, like Francis of Assisi, I must embrace the loathsome leper in order to see your face, your purpose in all things? Forgive me that my sins have kept so many bound in misery. And give me to think on what is lovely—and so help make it visible in all your creation. I ask in Jesus' holy name. AMEN.

Rejection Slips

Now therefore thus saith the Lord of hosts; Consider your ways. Ye have sown much, and bring in little; ye eat, but have not enough; ye drink, but ye are not filled with drink; ye clothe you, but there is none warm; and he that earneth wages earneth wages to put it into a bag with holes.

Haggai 1:5–6 (KJV)

He said to Simon, "Push the boat out further to the deep water, and you and your partners let your nets down for a catch." "Master," Simon answered, "we worked hard all night long and caught nothing. But if you say so, I will let down the nets." They let the nets down and caught such a large number of fish that the nets were about to break.

Luke 5:4–6 (TEV)

"Thank you for sending us your manuscript which we are returning herewith. We regret that it does not meet our immediate requirements."

Another rejection slip! In my efforts to get established

85

as a free-lance writer I'd acquired quite an assortment of them, enough to wallpaper the dining room, if I'd cared for a color scheme of white and yellow and pink.

It wasn't that I didn't know how to write. But I was writing the wrong things and sending them to the wrong places at the wrong time. Efforts to have my writing accepted for publication were as fruitless as Peter's efforts were fishless, until he followed the Lord's guidance.

O Heavenly Father, forgive me that I have thought I knew best about anything. That I thought I knew more than the all-knowing one. How foolish I've been. I do thank you that you have used my many failures to turn me to yourself, to teach me to trust in you. Like Peter, I've tried to argue that I'd done everything there was to do, when you have told me what you would have me do. And, when I've listened and been obedient, you have blessed me with an overflowing catch. Forgive all my reluctance to follow your leading and let me receive the abundant life you are so eager to give. I ask in Jesus' holy name. AMEN.

Not Look at Me!

Can a man hide himself in secret places so that I cannot see him? says the Lord. Do I not fill heaven and earth?

Jeremiah 23:24 (RSV)

"Not look at me!"

My child was vehement in his request. I was peering at him for something, probably trying to find out why he had done something wrong, or bad. I could understand his not wanting me to look at him, all out of sorts and in disgrace as he was. Why, I wouldn't have wanted anyone to look at me, either.

Dear God, I've never said, "Not look at me!" to you, but I've lived it. You've understood my thinking such a thought, when I had transgressed your laws and didn't want to acknowledge it before you. I've turned my back and pretended you were not there beside me through all

87

the turnings. I didn't look at you then, either. But you've always kept looking at me, and accepting me anyway, and loving me, and eventually I've turned again.

O Lord, forgive. Make me so aware of your loving, knowing presence within me that I'll know I cannot turn my back on your loving-kindness which is everywhere. Hallelujah! AMEN.

Communion

But God has shown us how much he loves us: it was while we were still sinners that Christ died for us!

Romans 5:8 (TEV)

We were late to church that morning, and I didn't know how far the service had progressed when we were ushered to our seats. A few pews ahead of me, I saw a man shake his head in refusal when something was passed. Was he indicating that he could not partake of communion? Did he think he was not righteous enough?

I was planning to partake of the communion emblems as usual. But his shaking head made me consider my own unrighteousness. How sorry I was for all the mistakes I had made in the week that had passed, all the sins that forgetting my Lord had occasioned. But I was there to remember him, to "do this in remembrance of me."

When the deacons came to our row I saw that it was

not a communion platter, but an offering tray they were passing. And as I passed it to my neighbor, I knew that all I *ever* have to give is my own unworthiness.

O Holy Father, how I do thank you that you do take even that—even my own unworthiness—and, because I offer it to you, do sanctify and clean me, making me whole to be your servant, recreating me again and again out of your perfect perfection. I thank you in all things, especially in that you did send your son to die for me, and that you do receive all prodigals, just as they are. And do richly bless them out of your abundance. AMEN.

A Friendly Call

Who shall ascend the hill of the Lord? And who shall stand in his holy place? He who has clean hands and a pure heart.

Psalm 24:3–4 (RSV)

Happy are the pure in heart: They will see God!

Matthew 5:8 (TEV)

I kept wondering why Elizabeth had called me. Because she had thirteen children, I was naturally suspicious at first. I supposed she wanted to borrow some money or have me help her find a new job. But no, to my every question she gave a more than satisfactory answer. She had a good job now, she said, made time-and-a-half all last week, working eleven hours a day at the factory. Her husband was working too. And all the children were well.

Then it came out. Elizabeth's landlord, the "rent man," as she called him, had been making some repairs and improvements on the house. She was happy about it and had been making some improvements herself, doing a little fixing-up. One of the improvements recently installed was a telephone. "Yes, I've got me a telephone now," she explained. "I jes' happened to be lookin' in the book and saw your name. And I thought I'd call."

That was it—it was just a social call. We talked a little longer, and then Elizabeth said, "You call *me* someday, and then I'll call you again."

I said, "Fine, I will," but I never did.

O Lord, forgive me, that I take so little time just for friendship. I always telephone with some special purpose in mind, never just to be friendly. And the world is so hungry for "just friendship," with no strings attached.

Deliver me from the misguided, mistaken self-importance that insists I must always be "accomplishing something." I do thank you for revealing my sins to me. Do change me, make me different—and new. In Jesus' name and for his sake. AMEN.

Rose Garden

But you, take courage! Do not let your hands be weak, for your work shall be rewarded.

2 *Chronicles* 15:7 (RSV)

On our fifteenth wedding anniversary my husband gave me a rose garden. At first glance it wasn't a very lovely thing. Neglected, unpruned, overgrown with crabgrass, nut grass, and wire grass, infested with Japanese beetles, blackspot, and weeds identifiable and otherwise, it boasted few perfect blossoms and an equal paucity of luxurious foliage.

It really wasn't much to look at, but I took it to heart. It needed me. We had just returned from a trip to visit my parents in Ohio. My father had spent several hours teaching me how to care for a rose garden, where to cut a bloom, how to prune the plants, which stalks would bring forth blossoms, and which should be cut down and cast into the fire.

And so I practiced what I had learned and harvested a great wheelbarrow load of dead and unproductive rose stalk, briars, and stems. There were a few blossoms which I put in hot water and refrigerated overnight so we might enjoy them on the breakfast table the next morning. That day, after supper, I went out again and weeded until my back could take it no longer. Already the plants looked better to me and more familiar. I was going to enjoy that bedraggled garden far more than I had enjoyed lovely roses cut and handed to me by other people. These roses *needed* me, and they were responding to my loving care.

I was responding to them, too, receiving healing in my spirit while I treated their ills. If they'd had no problems for me to help them with, I couldn't have come to know them very well or care as much when they prospered.

O Lord, thank you for giving me rose gardens—and friends. It's the same, somehow, with them, isn't it? If our friends had no problems for us to share, problems of cancer, or widowhood, or children failing in school, or the birth of a handicapped child, we'd not have become very well acquainted. By your grace, let all our troubles be ones that strengthen friendship, that knit the bonds of fellowship closer, that lead us nearer to you. In Jesus' name we ask. AMEN.

Poof!

But when thou art bidden, go and sit down in the lowest room.

Luke 14:10 (KJV)

Living with teenagers, I've discovered a need for the features found in some of the ancient castles—sliding panels, hidden doors, subterranean passageways. No, I'm not thinking of the times I need to make a getaway for my own salvation or find a perfect place to hide my last pair of nylons from a daughter who might "borrow" them, but—well, let me explain.

We were to have a meeting of a church youth group at our house. I had worked diligently, getting debris tucked out of sight, and the kitchen floor scrubbed, especially around the base of the baby's highchair where gooey evidences of breakfast scrambled eggs integrated unappetizingly with lunchtime peanut butter sandwich crumbs and blobs of mashed potatoes and salad greens from supper.

95

Somehow I managed to get things relatively orderly, shop for soft drinks enough to assuage the thirst of the mob, and bake numerous batches of butterscotch and chocolate brownies.

When all was in readiness, and I had rehabilitated my face, eager to greet the young people when they arrived, my eldest son approached me. He was clearing his throat in such a way as to alert me to the fact that he had something important to convey but wanted to appear casual about it. I listened intently, trying to look nonchalant and offhand about it. I didn't want to scare him off.

"You know, Mom," he began, "parents, well, like they're supposed to keep kind of in the background at these meetings. Not talk to people or do anything like that."

He looked me straight in the eye.

I nodded. Having been in circulation long enough to feel at ease with VIP's, I was bright enough to know that as a mother I was never supposed to speak to my kids' friends. Well, hardly ever.

Okay, so I wouldn't talk. But Tom looked as if there was more. Seeing that I had accepted his first bit of advice graciously enough, he brazened-up a bit to deliver the final blow:

"As a matter of fact, Mom," he went on, more sure of his ground—and his *rights*—"after they've served the refreshments, staying kind of in the background, the best parents just disappear!"

Poof! Like that, huh? Leaving maybe just a smidgen of a trail of smoke behind, maybe? No? Not even that?

I thought it but didn't say anything. I thought too about how the ancients were one up on us. Maybe half the secret panels and sliding doors were included in their architecture so that the best parents could serve the refreshments and then just disappear—poof!

Too modern for all that, I prepared a table for self-service of refreshments, snatched the baby up with one hand, plunked her in her stroller, and hoisted my umbrella for a two-hour walk in the rain.

Thank you, Lord, for showing me so much through the lives of my children, through what they say and do. Surely my self is supposed to disappear, not merely after I've served the refreshments, but all along. I am to grow so much like you that the obstreperous "I" will become invisible, having disappeared to let your life live in me and your way be known where we walk together. In Jesus' name I ask that it may be so with me. Amen.

Zzzzz

The time has come for you to wake up from your sleep. For the moment when we will be saved is closer now than it was when we first believed.

Romans 13:11 (TEV)

But they all alike began to make excuses.

Luke 14:18 (RSV)

I wasn't particularly aware of being sleepy as I drove the short distance to the hospital. I was going to pick up a friend and take her to her home, about fifteen miles out in the country. Usually I took my four-year-old daughter along with me, to keep me company on the ride back, but I didn't that day.

The ride out to Maizie's house was uneventful. She and I had lots to talk about. On the way home, however, I was aware, several times, of not being as wide awake as I ought to be—of finding myself unexplainably too close to the edge of the road—or the middle. I opened the window beside me, turned the heat off, and turned the radio on loud to keep me alert. It seemed to help—a little. And then, just a few blocks from home, I felt a sudden jolt. No, no one had hit me, but I had run up onto the curb in about the only place where I could have done it without running into a sign, a telephone pole, or some other obstruction.

My first thought as I turned the wheel to the left and returned to my proper lane in the street was of thankfulness that I'd hit no one, that I'd not had an accident, that no one had been hurt or killed by my negligence. There were other cars ahead of me, behind me, and some passing by, going in the other direction. How dangerous my driving had been to all of them! I should have stopped somewhere at the first sign of drowsiness and had some coffee or a soft drink and maybe some brisk walking-around to wake me up.

When I got to my house, I flopped down on the couch to see if a short nap would help. But my heart was beating too fast for sleep to come. And I found myself thinking how it must have looked—and felt—to the other motorists, when my car, obviously out of control, lurched up onto the sidewalk. And I thought, too, that it would have been good if I'd had my child along after all, because a toddler in the car would provide an excuse for my losing control of the car!

O Father, forgive my always wanting excuses, always wanting someone else to blame for my shortcomings, always wanting myself to look right. Burn away all impurity, refine me, make me pure in heart! AMEN.

See You Later

And when our mortality has been clothed with immortality, then the saying of Scripture will come true: 'Death is swallowed up; victory is won!' 'O death, where is your victory? O Death, where is your sting?'

1 Corinthians 15:54–55 (NEB)

The thank-you note was posted on the hall-way bulletin board at the eastern North Carolina School for the Deaf for all to read. "I thought flowers only cheered sick folks," it read. "But these did so much more. They gave me the support of my wonderful school family and the assurance that I would win the battle of such an unexpected operation. They dispelled fear. Have a happy Easter vacation. I look forward to seeing you afterwards. Love, Jane Chase."

Mrs. Chase was the much loved principal of Vestal Hall. I became acquainted with her when I helped catalog

101

some books for the children's library there. I had known her just a little while when she was admitted to the hospital for surgery from which she made such a marvelous recovery. Oh yes, they buried her body, but she had blessed assurance that she would win the battle. Her fear was dispelled. She believed in the resurrection. She looked forward to seeing us afterward. How could there be room for defeat in the midst of such faith as that?

O Father, we are so thankful for your gift of eternal life to all who receive your Son. We are so thankful for the love that casts out fear, for the victory over pain. Plant them deep within us that we may never lose heart. In the name of Jesus Christ, our risen Lord we pray. AMEN.

Truth Will Out

There is nothing covered up that will not be uncovered, nothing hidden that will not be made known.

Matthew 10:26 (NEB)

It was just after lunch and I had unceremoniously dumped two-thirds of my little tribe in bed for their afternoon naps. Tommy was staying up to "help" me get the house ready for company expected later that afternoon. We had succeeded in straightening the tiny living room and in getting the dining room lunch debris shoved into the kitchen for further attention when the doorbell rang.

Impeccable, as usual, in black suit and gray derby hat, Mr. Silas Lucas had been out taking his "constitutional" and decided to drop by for a visit. I was clad in my customary uniform too—faded blue jeans and a shirt that bore smudges of pablum and other less readily identifiable glop. But it could have been worse. At least the living

103

room was straight, so I relaxed and sat down with my husband to enjoy the intelligent adult conversation. Mr. Lucas always used words of at least four syllables, and the mind-stretching was good for me. I tried to be a little polysyllabic myself.

After a few minutes Tommy asked if he could whisper something in my ear. Assuming the message had something to do with bathrooming, I consented.

But what he said was, "Mama, doesn't he have *huge feet!*"

If he'd said it aloud, it might have been slightly embarrassing, but we'd all have laughed and it would have been all right and forgotten in a little while. Maybe Mr. Lucas would have tucked his feet out of sight under his chair, or something.

But Tommy's message came to my ears alone, and I had some difficulty controlling my eyes, which wanted to stare at the whoppers stuck out into the middle of the 9 x 12 rug that served as almost wall-to-wall carpet.

The rest of the conversation was lost on me. I became utterly monosyllabic, trying to keep from bursting into a guffaw at those boats of his. Then I had to excuse myself, on the pretext of checking on the little baby.

When I returned to the living room, I heard Mr. Lucas and my husband talking in the kitchen. I remembered, without looking, that there were clean clothes on the washer, dirty ones on the floor, dirty dishes and food scraps in jumbled disarray everywhere else. I was too undone to face him and retreated to the bedroom, knowing he'd soon forget the neat living room but would hold forever in his memory the picture of the sloppiest kitchen in Wilson.

O Father, why do I have to pretend perfection that can never be? From how high an estate do I think I have come to suppose that my kitchen could ever be presentable for company? Forgive my unreasonable standards for myself—and for other people. Let me credit all others with the intelligence to know what living is and mostly make me as uncritical of others as I want them to be of me. I ask for Jesus' sake. AMEN.

Ironing Bored

I am your Lord and Teacher, and I have just washed your feet.
You, then, should wash each other's feet. I have set an example
for you, so that you will do just what I have done for you. I tell
you the truth: no slave is greater than his master; no messenger
is greater than the one who sent him. Now you know this truth;
how happy you will be if you put it into practice!

John 13:14–17 (TEV)

I had expected someone to come to help with
the ironing that day. But she hadn't showed up. There
was a heaping basket of clothes to get ready for vacation
packing. Eight people in the family makes lots of laundry
chores—always.

So I got out the iron and the ironing board and began.
It wasn't easy, trying to keep up with the two babies by
myself and to bear the burden of thinking about all the
other things that had to be done before we could leave the

next day. The older children, who could have helped, were still in school.

As I ironed, I complained inwardly at having to do such a routine, menial, time-consuming job when more important things commanded my attention, things that someone else could not do for me.

But wait a minute! In the middle of my fuming, my eye glanced upon the little *Good News for Modern Man* open on a bamboo stand beside the kitchen sink. Who had turned it to *that* page? There was a picture of one, kneeling, with a towel around his waist, a basin at his side. The Lord and Savior of all the world was washing Peter's feet.

O my dear Heavenly Father, forgive my foolish self-importance. Burst the balloon of my puffed up pride. Make me humble to know that as you did send your precious Son to take upon himself the sin of the world—my sin—that no task is too low, too insignificant, too trivial for me. I fume no more, but thank you that you have made me a mother to serve your children, to ready for them clean places to sleep, good food to eat, smooth clothes to wear—and to wash their feet. And I thank you that no other came to help, but that you showed me yourself. AMEN.

Fall Out

But one thing I do, forgetting what lies behind and straining forward to what lies ahead, I press on toward the goal for the prize of the upward call of God in Christ Jesus.

Philippians 3:13–14 (RSV)

Dino was just past a year old when he and his big sister, all of two-and-a-half, were playing out in the yard together. Alice was pushing him in his stroller, circling the house, safe because the yard was fenced on all sides. She was pushing fast, and she and Dino were chuckling in great glee every time I saw them pass the kitchen window.

Then suddenly I looked out and saw Alice, still laughing hilariously, flying along with an *empty* stroller.

I hadn't heard any crying, but I flew outside as fast as I could. "Where's Dino?" I cried, as Alice whizzed past me.

"Oh, he fell out," she said, completely unconcerned as

she continued on her merry way. I found him happily pasturing on the green grass on the other side of the house, just as matter-of-fact about his predicament as she was.

O Lord, I confess that I have been just like Alice. I begin something that has a good purpose in it, and gleefully set to work, enjoying every minute of it. But when somewhere along the line the purpose falls out, as it does sometimes, I go blithely along as if the purpose never mattered to begin with. Make me mindful of serving you, of your purpose in all things. Keep me alert to see that your purpose remains and is fulfilled. I thank you. AMEN.

Pet Peeves

Let there be no more resentment, no more anger or temper, no more violent self-assertiveness, no more slander and no more malicious remarks. Be kind to one another; be understanding. Be as ready to forgive others as God for Christ's sake has forgiven you.

Ephesians 4:31–32 (Phillips)

Pet peeves. Everyone recognizes the expression. And probably, if a man was asked to name his pet peeve, he would have to sort through a whole list of them to pick out the really worst one. And how often our pet peeve begins, "My pet peeve is people who—" And whether the rest of it has to do with aggravations with people for not putting the top back on the toothpaste, or not staying within the painted lines in a parking space, or using so much perfume that those forced to work around them are nearly asphyxiated, our pet peeves are invariably directed against people. Even when the pet peeve seems to be

111

directed at an inanimate object we are really aggravated at the person behind it—the designer who made a box that won't open readily, the postal employees who don't expedite the mail as we think they ought, etc. People are behind most of what we complain about.

But how we cherish our pet peeves. The very name suggests how we pet them, caress them, nourish them into health and long life. Why we wouldn't give up our pet peeves for anything!

O Lord, forgive me my pet peeves against people. Why, you loved people so much that you sent your only Son to die to save them! Forgive how I have relished and cherished and fed my resentments against those who don't do things the way I do, who don't see things with my perspective. You know I have a whole drawer full of slights and misgivings I can bring out to air at will. Make me clean out the bureaus of my soul, emptying the ugly collections of unkind thoughts, and fill the spaces with your beauty. For your love's sake I ask it. AMEN.

Dress Rehearsal

So do not worry about tomorrow; it will have enough worries of
its own.

Matthew 6:34 (TEV)

We thought our first red-headed daughter
was a reasonably well-adjusted child until we began to
take her to Sunday school. I couldn't figure it out. Every
Sunday morning we'd leave her in the nursery, perfectly
happy as she went in to play with the other three-year-olds,
the puzzles, the housekeeping equipment and the doll
babies. And every Sunday, two hours later when we went
to get her, we'd have to rescue our screaming child from
the arms of someone who had been trying unsuccessfully
to comfort her. What was the matter?

One Sunday morning I found out. We were just finishing our preparations to leave the house when I found Alice
standing in a corner. As she rolled and unrolled her father's

belt, one of her favorite toys, she rehearsed aloud: "No, thank you; please don't pick me up; no, thank you; please don't pick me up."

That day I told the nursery attendants about what I had observed and suggested that they not pick her up, and we'd see if that helped what had become a difficult situation for us all. There were no cries of distress when we went down the hall after church. For the first time Alice had stayed happy the whole two hours.

Father, do I sometimes cause others great distress by my pushing too close? Do they come to dread my appearance because I will try to smother them in affection they do not welcome? Forgive me. Teach me to respect all the independence I see, in others or in my own children. Let me suffer them to come to me, out of their need, not make them suffer by inflicting hovering comforting that does not comfort. And help Alice, and others like her, not to add to their own distress by worrying about troubles ahead of time. In Jesus' name. AMEN.

Patience, Patience

My brethren, count it all joy when ye fall into divers temptations; Knowing this, that the trying of your faith worketh patience. But let patience have her perfect work, that ye may be perfect and entire, wanting nothing.

James 1:2–4 (KJV)

For ye have need of patience, that, after ye have done the will of God, ye might receive the promise.

Hebrews 10:36 (KJV)

In your patience possess ye your souls.

Luke 21:19 (KJV)

Do you ever read your "no-class-mail"? The kind that comes without your asking for it, I mean. Advertisements and all that stuff. I don't usually read mine either, but one letter caught my eye the other day. It was a fund solicitation, of course—most of them are, one way or another—and it began with a poem. The author was not named and I've long since lost the letter, but maybe I can quote it sufficiently for you to get the drift. It went something like this:

> Plant patience in the garden of thy soul.
> The root is bitter, but the fruit is sweet
> And when at last it stands, a tree complete
> The burning heat and problems of the day
> Will lose control—
> Plant patience in the garden of thy soul.

O Lord, I confess that I've had a wrong notion of what patience is. I've thought it was the "I'll-be-patient-if-it-kills-me" that I muttered through tight lips while I ground my teeth to nubbins and strained my arteries until they were ready to pop—the kind of patience that would be spelled "cardiac" on my death certificate.

Who's been the boss of my life? Me? Or my problems? Most days, the problems. I confess it.

O Lord, forgive me that I have been so impatient. Cultivate my soul, by your grace, that true patience planted may take root there and find nourishment to grow into your patience, the patience of peace that passes all understanding. In whatever circumstances I find myself. In Jesus' holy name. AMEN.

What Time Is It?

It is the time to seek the Lord, that he may come and rain salvation upon you.

Hosea 10:12 (RSV)

But do not forget this one thing, my dear friends! There is no difference in the Lord's sight between one day and a thousand years; to him the two are the same.

2 Peter 3:8 (TEV)

I am forever amazed and amused at children's peculiar concept of time. They are always counting, always wondering: "How many more days till Christmas?" "Is tomorrow in the morning?" "Is in the morning when we wake up?" "Is it today now?"

I remember reminding one of the little ones to go to the bathroom before we got in the car to make a trip. He informed me, most indignantly, that he had used the bathroom when Ann Messick was here! That was just fine, so he had, but she was living in another state and he hadn't seen her for at least two years!

What is it Lord? Do children partake of eternity with you? Is that why time is so different for them? Why it is so hard to make them hurry, and so impossible to make them wait? Is life all-at-once to a child? And is that why they can be so close to you? What agonies they avoid that way, agonies that nearly consume us grownups looking at our watches every few minutes to make sure we're going to be on time about something.

Make me as a little child, now, then. I would be seeking you at all times and in all places, and serving others as I go. In Jesus' name I ask it. AMEN.

Success

Who, then, can separate us from the love of Christ? Can trouble do it, or hardship, or persecution, or hunger, or poverty, or danger, or death? No, in all these things we have complete victory through him who loved us! For I am certain that nothing can separate us from his love: neither death nor life; neither angels nor other heavenly rulers or powers; neither the present nor the future; neither the world above nor the world below—there is nothing in all creation that will ever be able to separate us from the love of God which is ours through Christ Jesus our Lord.

Romans 8:35, 37–39 (TEV)

Emily Dickinson has a little poem which goes:

> Success is counted sweetest
> By those who ne'er succeed.
> To comprehend a nectar
> Requires sorest need.
>
> Not one of all the purple host
> Who took the flag to-day

Can tell the definition,
So clear, of victory,

As he defeated, dying,
On whose forbidden ear
The distant strains of triumph
Break, agonized and clear.

I think she's right that success is counted sweetest by those who don't succeed. A goal unreached seems still a prize worthy to be sought. But I don't agree that it's the dying, defeated man, the one who did not attain the goal, who knows the true meaning of victory better than the one who achieved it. It is the man who achieves worldly victory who knows its true worth—which isn't so great after all. Worldly victory, an earthly prize, is never what it's cracked up to be. But only those who have drawn near enough to grasp it know it.

O Lord, how many things I have sought in this life that I thought were the "be-all and know-all," the supreme height and achievement. And how wrong I've been every single time. Give me to know where true worth lies, and to seek you above all else. Let me count success as being won by you, as being one with you. And keep me close to truth, ever pursuing. I ask, and I thank you, in Jesus' holy name. Amen.

Believing the *Unbelievable*

Woe unto them who call evil good, and good evil; that put
darkness for light, and light for darkness; that put bitter for sweet,
and sweet for bitter!

Isaiah 5:20 (KJV)

Ten years ago, on a sunny June afternoon, I
left my husband in charge of our four little ones while I
went to the grocery store and did other errands about town.
It being such a beautiful day, and he being a father who
loved to see his children enjoy themselves, Allen set up our
little inflatable wading pool and filled it with water. While
the water warmed in the sunshine, the kids donned their
bathing suits. They had a splashing good time for several
hours.

You have already guessed that there were some signs
of reddened shoulders when we pajamaed the kids for bed
later that day. By morning, my youngest redhead, whose

skin was pale and sensitive to begin with, woke up with the biggest, bulgiest blisters I'd ever seen—absolutely unbelievable.

His big brother, all of five years old, took one incredulous look, shook his head and said reassuringly, "Maybe it's just applesauce."

O Lord, how lightly I, too, dismiss evils so evil I can't believe them. "Oh, it's probably just my imagination," I say, certain that no one could be that bad. Or, seeing pictures of families living in terrible poverty and impossible filth I disclaim responsibility with, "Well, they're probably used to it and it doesn't bother them as much as it would me."

O God, most merciful, stir my conscience to acknowledge the reality of evil in the world—and show me what to do, how to love, to eliminate it, to keep it from happening in future generations. For your love's sake I ask it. AMEN.

So Let It Be Written—
So Let It Be Done

Do your best to present yourself to God as one approved, a workman who has no need to be ashamed.

2 Timothy 2:15(RSV)

Let all things be done decently and in order.

1 Corinthians 14:40 (KJV)

For God is not a God of disorder but of order.

1 Corinthians 14:33 (Williams)

Years ago, when our teenagers were toddlers, I found myself frustrated frequently because I could not find a pencil or any other writing instrument in the house. The lack always came to my attention when I had some vital thought or insight to record in words too precious to lose.

After a long time, during which many immortal phrases

123

were lost, I adopted various insurance measures against the same thing happening again—ever. No, I didn't provide myself with two closets full of sharpened pencils. In our household they'd have evaporated overnight. Nor did I lay in a supply of fountain pens and a few gallons of ink. I'd have had to wash *that* out of diapers and dungarees, the way things went. I did have a typewriter, but ribbons invariably wound up twined around teddy bears when my back was turned for a second.

No, instead, I learned to leave a few windows deliberately dirty so that a moistened fingertip could code the initial letters of words born into a precious sequence. And I left unerased a child's scrawled-full chalkboard so I could make black tracks upon it that I might decipher on a legible tomorrow when the wherewithal for writing could be borrowed from my husband's coat pocket as he walked in the door.

Sometimes there were crayons and pencils galore. Only then there'd be no paper to use them on. One year I resorted to crayoned notes on the refrigerator door. Such notes never got lost, but the glossy finish of the refrigerator dulled substantially and I was forced to paint it. The hold of the new paint over the rust spots was so tenuous I hardly dared wipe it with a damp cloth to remove the inevitably omnipresent grubby finger prints, let alone scour writing away.

One day, when writing instruments and paper were simultaneously lacking, one of the kids brought in an egg-sized lump of coal from somewhere. I used it on the margins of yesterday's newspapers but never was able to figure out what the smudges meant later.

O Lord, all that sounds ridiculous now, years later when our home abounds with writing instruments everywhere I look. But there's still never a pencil within reach of the telephone when there's an urgent message or phone number to record. I have tied a pencil nearby, lots of times. Only someone—generally me—usually borrows it for something and forgets to return it.

And it isn't just pencils. Before-school-mornings are sometimes spoiled because the boys can't find any pairs of clean socks to wear—I've failed to finish up the laundry and put it away where they can find it. Or the girls have to remind me a dozen times when a skirt needs hemming or slip straps need attention.

O Lord, I know I'm busy, there are lots of things to do, but you have given me common sense about what ought to be done to avoid such foolish frustrations. I thank you for common sense. Now, by your grace, make me use it. Let me not waste time in unfruitful pursuits but let me work to smooth our lives that we all might serve you better. In Jesus' name. AMEN.